CONTINENTS

Europe

Leila Merrell Foster

Heinemann Library
Chicago, Illinois

Designed by Depke Design
Printed and bound in China by South China Printing Company.

06 05
10 9 8 7

Library of Congress Cataloging-in-Publication Data
Foster, Leila Merrell.
   Europe / Leila Merrell Foster.
      p. cm. -- (Continents)
   Includes bibliographical references and index.
   ISBN 1-57572-213-5 (lib. bdg.)   ISBN 1-58810-949-6 (pbk. bdg.)
   1. Europe--Juvenile literature. [1. Europe.] I. Title. II. Continents (Chicago, Ill.)
D1051 .F67 2001
940--dc21   00-011468

Acknowledgments
The publishers are grateful to the following for permission to reproduce copyright material: Bruce Coleman, Inc./Lee Foster, p. 5; Earth Scenes/P. O'Toole, p. 7; Photo Edit/Tony Freeman, p. 9; Tony Stone/Shaun Egan, p. 11; Bruce Coleman, Inc./Olivier Lequeinec, p. 13; Animals Animals/Darek Karp, p. 14; Bruce Coleman, Inc./Wedlgo Ferchland, p. 15; Corbis/Tony Arruza, p. 16; Tony Stone/Michael Busselle, p. 17; Photo Edit/Amy Etra, p. 19; Bruce Coleman, Inc./Masha Nor dbye, p. 20; Tony Stone/John Lamb, p. 21; Bruce Coleman, Inc./Guido Cozzi, pp. 22, 25; Bruce Coleman, Inc./C. & J. McClurg, p. 24; Tony Stone/Arnold Husmo, p. 26; Bruce Coleman, Inc., p. 27; Photo Edit/Bill Buchmann, p. 28.

 Every effort has been made to contact copyright holders of any material reproduced in this book. Any omissions will be rectified in subsequent printings if notice is given to the publisher.

Some words are shown in bold, **like this.**
You can find out what they mean by looking in the glossary.

Contents

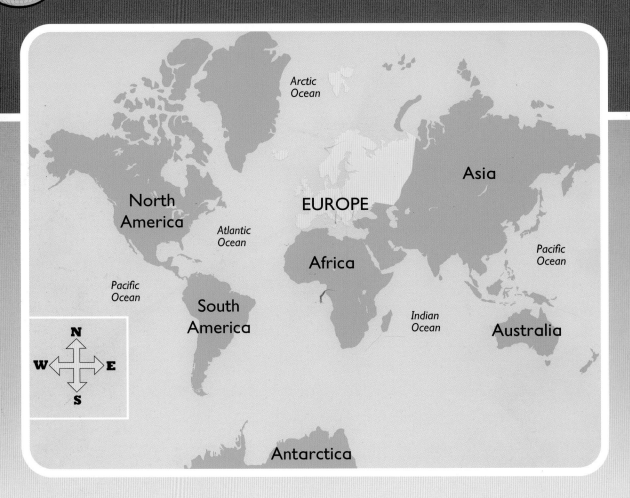

There are seven continents in the world. Europe is the second smallest continent. To the north of Europe is the Arctic Ocean. To the west is the Atlantic Ocean.

Fjords near Harstad, Norway

Europe is connected to the much larger continent of Asia. Because it developed differently than Asia, it is called a continent.

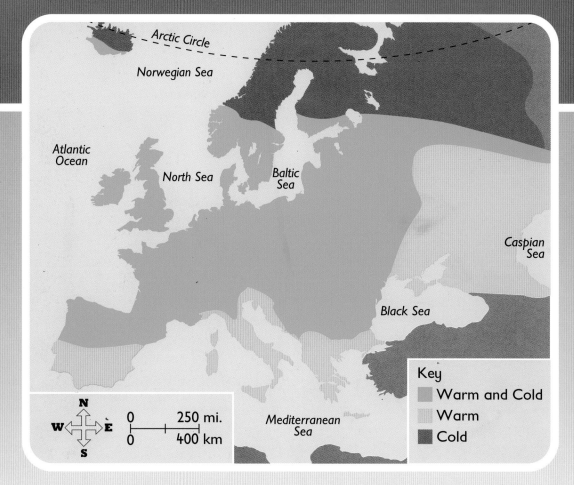

Arctic Circle
Norwegian Sea
Atlantic Ocean
North Sea
Baltic Sea
Caspian Sea
Black Sea
Mediterranean Sea

N
W
E
S

0   250 mi.
0   400 km

Key
Warm and Cold
Warm
Cold

All of Europe is north of the **equator**. Some parts of Europe lie north of the **Arctic Circle**. This is why Europe has many different **climates**.

Glen Etive, Scotland

Areas of western Europe get lots of rain. The temperatures are **mild** all year. In the north, there is less rain and long, cold winters.

Mountains

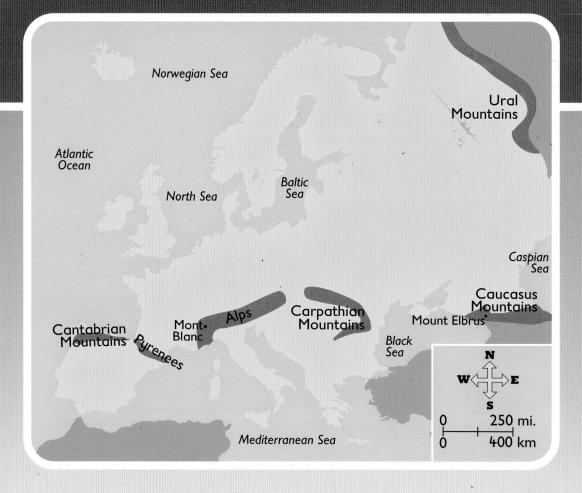

The highest mountain in Europe is Mount Elbrus. It is in the Caucasus Mountains. These mountains lie between the continents of Europe and Asia.

Jungfrau Peak, Swiss Alps

The Alps are in southern Europe. They stretch across the continent from east to west. Mont Blanc is a high mountain in this **range.**

Rivers

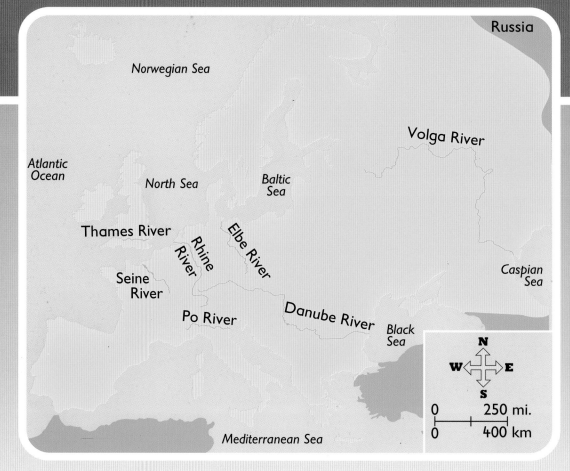

Russia

Norwegian Sea

Volga River

Atlantic Ocean

North Sea

Baltic Sea

Thames River

Rhine River

Elbe River

Caspian Sea

Seine River

Po River

Danube River

Black Sea

Mediterranean Sea

N
W — E
S

0   250 mi.
0   400 km

The longest river in Europe is the Volga River. It
flows through Russia to the Caspian Sea. This river
is usually frozen for three months each year.

Danube River, Budapest, Hungary

The Danube is an important river in Europe. It flows from west to east and empties into the Black Sea. Ships and **barges** carry people and **goods** to cities on the Danube.

Lakes

Norwegian Sea

Lake Onega

Lake Ladoga

Baltic Sea

Lake Peipus

Atlantic Ocean

Lake Vänern

Lake Vättern

North Sea

Caspian Sea

Lake Geneva

Lake of Lucerne

Lake Balaton

Black Sea

N
W E
S

0   250 mi.
0   400 km

Mediterranean Sea

Europe's largest **freshwater** lake is Lake Ladoga. Its water is yellowish-brown. Many fish live there.

Lake Geneva, Switzerland

Switzerland has many beautiful lakes, such as Lake Geneva and Lake of Lucerne. They are near mountain **ranges.** Many people use these lakes for sailing and other fun things.

Animals

Gray Wolf in Poland

Many kinds of animals in Europe have almost disappeared. People have hunted these animals for thousands of years. For example, very few wolves live in Europe.

Reindeer in Sweden

In the north, people herd reindeer. Reindeer provide meat, milk, and fur. People move their reindeer to different places in winter and summer to find food for them.

Plants

Olive trees in Spain

Farmers in Italy and Spain grow much of the world's olive trees. The fruit of the olive tree is eaten whole or crushed to make cooking oil. Some olive trees live for hundreds of years.

16

Vineyard, Loire, France

Europe is famous for its grapes that are crushed to make juice and wine. Good **soil** and the perfect **climate** make grape growing easy in some parts of Europe.

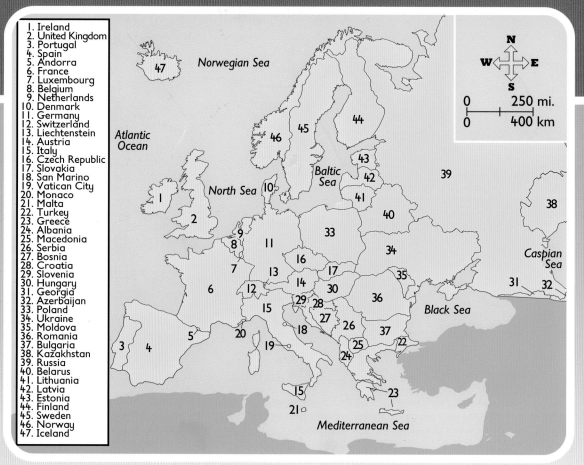

1. Ireland
2. United Kingdom
3. Portugal
4. Spain
5. Andorra
6. France
7. Luxembourg
8. Belgium
9. Netherlands
10. Denmark
11. Germany
12. Switzerland
13. Liechtenstein
14. Austria
15. Italy
16. Czech Republic
17. Slovakia
18. San Marino
19. Vatican City
20. Monaco
21. Malta
22. Turkey
23. Greece
24. Albania
25. Macedonia
26. Serbia
27. Bosnia
28. Croatia
29. Slovenia
30. Hungary
31. Georgia
32. Azerbaijan
33. Poland
34. Ukraine
35. Moldova
36. Romania
37. Bulgaria
38. Kazakhstan
39. Russia
40. Belarus
41. Lithuania
42. Latvia
43. Estonia
44. Finland
45. Sweden
46. Norway
47. Iceland

There are 47 countries in Europe. Most countries have one **official** language. Many Europeans speak several languages. They might speak English, French, or German besides their own language.

Outdoor newsstand, Rome, Italy

About 60 different languages are spoken in Europe. Some languages have letters different from those in English.

Kremlin, Moscow, Russia

Moscow is the biggest city in Europe. The leaders of Russia work in a place called the Kremlin. Parts of the Kremlin are more than 500 years old.

London, England

London is one of the world's most important cities. Many famous scientists and writers have lived there.

Acropolis, Athens, Greece

Athens was once the most powerful city in the world. People throughout the world still follow the ideas of the great leaders and thinkers of **ancient** Athens.

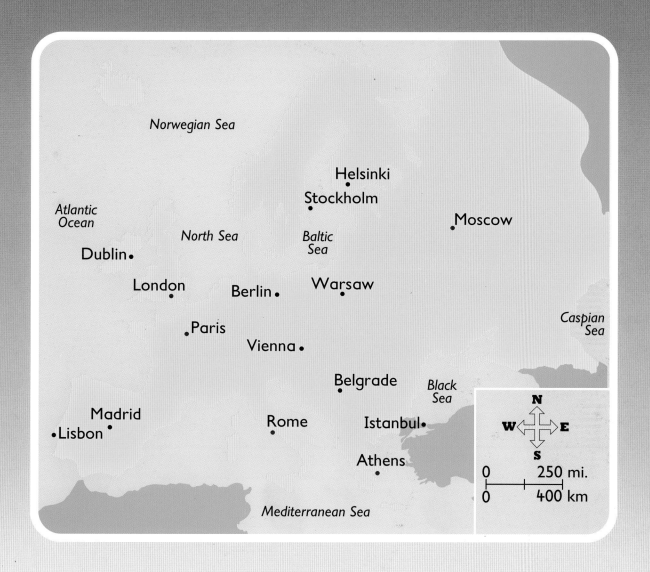

Norwegian Sea

Helsinki

Stockholm

Atlantic Ocean

North Sea

Baltic Sea

Moscow

Dublin

London

Berlin

Warsaw

Paris

Vienna

Caspian Sea

Belgrade

Black Sea

Madrid

Rome

Istanbul

Lisbon

Athens

N
W E
S

0   250 mi.
0   400 km

Mediterranean Sea

Paris, France, is a city with many museums and beautiful churches. It is famous for its schools and artists. Famous clothes **designers** like to live and work in Paris.

Lisbon, Portugal

Europe has good **ports** for fishing boats. Fishing is an important business along the **coasts** of many countries.

Odense, Denmark

Farmers in many countries use modern machines. These farmers grow much of the food that they and their neighbors eat. They also sell food to other countries.

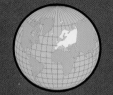

Troll Fjord, Norway

Fjords with tall, rocky walls cut into the western **coast** of Europe. Large ships can sail far inland because the water is so deep.

Colosseum, Rome, Italy

The Colosseum was built by the Romans almost 2,000 years ago. It was used for sporting events. Soccer is the most popular sport in Europe today.

Eiffel Tower, Paris, France

The Eiffel Tower is one of the most famous places in the world. It was built to show how steel could be used in very tall buildings. More than five million people visit it each year.

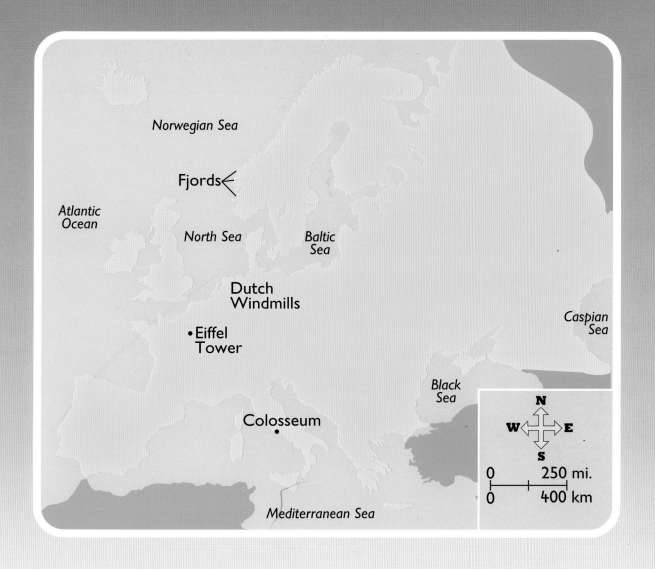

Norwegian Sea

Fjords

Atlantic
Ocean

North Sea

Baltic
Sea

Dutch
Windmills

Caspian
Sea

•Eiffel
Tower

Black
Sea

Colosseum

N
W E
S

0   250 mi.
0   400 km

Mediterranean Sea

Dutch windmills were once very important. They were used to pump water from fields that flooded. Wind turns the large blades of the windmills to make power.

1. Europe makes more goods than any other continent.

2. The world's largest lake, the Caspian Sea, lies partly in Europe.

3. Finland has 60,000 lakes and is known as the "land of thousands of lakes."

4. Most of Europe gets from 20 to 60 inches (50 to 150 centimeters) of rain each year.

5. The St. Gotthard Road Tunnel in central Switzerland is the world's longest motor traffic tunnel (10.1 miles, 16.3 kilometers).

6. More than half the land in Europe is used for farming.

7. Europe has the largest country in the world, Russia, and the smallest country in the world, Vatican City.

8. Rotterdam, in the Netherlands, is one of the busiest ports in the world.

Glossary

ancient something from a very long time ago

Arctic Circle imaginary line that circles the earth near the North Pole

barge large boat with a flat bottom, used to carry heavy loads

climate kind of weather a place has

coast land right next to water

designer person who thinks of something new

equator imaginary circle around the exact middle of the earth

fjords long, skinny waterways that are deep and flow far inland

freshwater water that is not salty

goods things that people buy and use

mild warm, but not hot

official having to do with a government or leader

port place where ships load and unload cargo

range line of connected mountains

soil dirt in which plants grow

More Books to Read

McLeish, Ewan. *Europe*. Austin, Tex.: Raintree Steck-Vaughn Pub., 1997.

Petersen, David. *Europe*. Danbury, Conn.: Children's Press, 1998.

Sammis, Fran. *Europe & the Middle East*. Tarrytown, N.Y.: Marshall Cavendish Corp., 1998.

Index